WHAT'S BEST FOR
MY BABY
AND ME?

A Three-Step Guide for Parents

BY CLAIRE LERNER AND
AMY LAURA DOMBRO

ZERO
TO
THREE®

Washington, [

D1052581

Published by

ZERO
TO
THREE

National Center for Infants,
Toddlers and Families

ZERO TO THREE
2000 M St., NW, Suite 200
Washington, DC 20036-3307
(202) 638-1144
Toll-free orders (800) 899-4301
Fax: (202) 638-0851
Web: http://www.zerotothree.org

The mission of the ZERO TO THREE Press is to publish authoritative research, practical
resources, and new ideas for those who work with and care about infants, toddlers, and their
families. Books are selected for publication by an independent Editorial Board. The views con-
tained in this book are those of the authors and do not necessarily reflect those of ZERO TO
THREE: National Center for Infants, Toddlers and Families, Inc.

Design: Metze Publication Design

Library of Congress Cataloging-in-Publication Data

Lerner, Claire.
  What's best for my baby and me? : a 3-step guide for parents / by
Claire Lerner and Amy Laura Dombro.-- 1st ed.
     p. cm.
  Adaptation of the authors' Bringing up baby. c2004.
  ISBN 0-943657-94-6
  1. Child rearing. 2. Parenting. 3. Infants--Care. 4. Infants--
Development. 5. Child development. I. Dombro, Amy Laura,
1953- II. Lerner, Claire. Bringing up baby. III. Title.
  HQ769.L387 2005
  649'.122--dc22

                                                              2005036111

10 9 8 7 6 5 4 3 2 1
ISBN 0-943657-94-6
Printed in the United States of America

Suggested citation:
Book citation: Lerner, C., & Dombro, A. L. (2006). What's best for my baby and
me?:
A 3-step guide for parents. Washington, DC: ZERO TO THREE Press.

Contents

Introduction

Raising a young child means making decisions: Can I let my baby cry? For how long? Should I let my toddler watch TV? What kind of discipline is best? The list never ends.

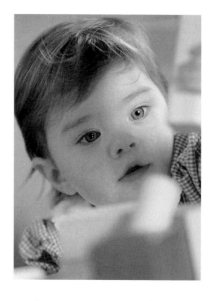

Like most parents, you are probably looking for answers. However, there is no such thing as a one-size-fits-all approach to parenting. Since we don't know you, your child, or the world you share, what good would our advice be?

So this book does not tell you how to raise your child. We don't tell you how to get your baby to sleep or how to get your toddler to use the potty. Instead, this book describes a three-step plan to help *you* solve everyday parenting problems. Here are the three steps:

Step 1: Know yourself. Think about your own feelings and reactions as a parent and how they affect your child.

Step 2: Know your child. Try to understand what your child is thinking and feeling. Ask, "What does his behavior mean?

Step 3: Make sensitive and effective decisions. Use what you know about yourself (Step1) and your child (Step 2) to make good decisions.

In the pages that follow, you will find:

- **Information on child development**

- **Stories about families and children**

- **Questions and other tools to think and talk about with other adults in your child's life.**

As you read, you will see that you know a lot about how to raise your child. And, that you are your own best resource when it comes to making decisions that make sense for you, your child, and your family.

Step 1

Know Yourself

We begin with you. Why? Because you are the most important person in your child's life. Every day you have the chance to help her:

- feel safe and secure

- explore and learn

- feel self-confident

- learn to control her behavior

- learn how to make friends

Here are two stories of parents helping their children grow up healthy:

When Sasha (20 months) would cling to me in the child-care center, I wanted to run away. Then I realized she needed my help to get settled. So now I read a book with her before I leave. Just yesterday, while I was reading, she got up and went over to play with the other kids.

When Rubin (26 months) is having a knock-down-drag-out tantrum, he pulls it together much more quickly when I stay calm and comfort him. Now Rubin's tantrums are shorter and happen less often.

Think about how you help your child grow up healthy every day

- What are some things you did with (or for) your child today?

- What do you think your child learned from these experiences?

- What made your child laugh? What made you laugh?

- What do you think was your child's favorite moment? Why?

Three Key Factors That Influence How You Parent

There are three key factors that influence how you parent:

- Your hopes and fears for your child
- Your own childhood experiences
- Your personal style

Your Expectations for Your Child

All parents have dreams for their child. One mom wants her son to be a musician. A dad wants his daughter to be a scientist.

Parents also have worries. One dad, who had trouble in school, is concerned that his child will have trouble too. A mom wonders if her son, who looks like her brother, will have a drinking problem just like him.

When you know your hopes and fears, you can put them aside. You can see your child for who he really is. You can respond to *his* personality and *his* interests.

Think about your expectations for your child

- Before your baby was born, what did you think she would be like?

- How is your child similar to what you had hoped? How is he different?

Your Childhood Experiences

Your experiences as a child play a big part in how you respond to your child. For example, a dad splashes in puddles with his son because he loved doing this with his dad.

Sometimes parents choose to do the opposite of what their own parents did. For example, one mom decides not to make her child eat every bite of food on his plate because her mother forced her to do so. Growing up in our families, we learned lots of things:

- **How to feel about ourselves** such as good, bad, smart, dumb, pretty, unattractive, lovable, or difficult.

- **How people get along with each other** such as with warmth or anger.

- **How to express anger** such as by talking, shouting, or hitting.

- **How to get children to behave** such as by showing them how to behave, praising them for good behavior, yelling, or taking things away.

Think about how your childhood experiences affect what you say to and do with your child

- How did your mother, father, or other loved ones help you feel good about yourself and your abilities? What did they say and do? Do you say or do things with your child that are similar? Different?

- Were there ways that family members made you feel bad about yourself? What did they do and say? Do you do and say things to your child that are similar? Different?

- Are there changes you want to make in the messages you send to your child? Which ones? Why?

Your Own Personal Style

We each have our own way of approaching and reacting to things. This is our **temperament**. For example, some people may be uncomfortable in new places or meeting new people. Others jump right into new situations. Some people are very intense. Others are more laid-back.

Your temperament affects your interactions with your child. For example, if you are an outgoing person, it might be difficult to have a child who is shy. You may have to slow down for her.

Here is an example of a dad who is adjusting to his child's temperament:

Kevin, an outgoing person, takes his daughter Tyra (11 months) to the park. She starts to cry when a group of toddlers joins her in the sandbox. She reaches for Kevin. He picks her up and comforts her. But then Kevin goes a step further. When Tyra calms down, he sits at her side by the sandbox, talking and playing with her. Soon Tyra is creeping closer to watch the other kids.

Kevin does not force Tyra to be outgoing like he is. He supports her. Then he helps her feel comfortable in this situation.

Nobody's Perfect—And You Don't Have to Be!

Parents learn as they go. If something you try doesn't work, then try something else.

Here is how a mom learns by trial and error:

had tried everything to help Sharif (15 months) calm down when he was upset. The harder I tried, the more upset he got. One day, I ran out of ideas. I gave Shariff time in his room where I knew he'd be safe. Five minutes later I peeked in. He was happily looking at books. What he needed all along was space and time to calm down on his own.

Think of a time when you made a mistake or tried something that didn't work

- What did you learn?

- What will you try next time? Why?

Take Care of Yourself

All parents feel overwhelmed at times. It is very important to know when you need to take a break or ask for help. You will take better care of your baby when you are taken care of and supported.

Think about how to take care of yourself

- How do you know when you need a break?

- Who can you call for support?

- What do you do to take care of yourself?

- How can you make time for you?

REMEMBER

- You are the most important person in your child's life. What you do with and say to her matters a lot!

- Think before you act. It will help you understand the situation better and come up with new ideas for how to respond.

- Nobody is perfect. You can learn from your mistakes.

- Take care of yourself. It will help you be an even better parent.

Step **2**

Know Your Child

Why does your child behave the way he does? What does his behavior mean? When you understand your child's behavior, you can respond in ways that help his healthy development.

Being a Detective

Figuring out the meaning of your child's behavior is like being a detective. You look for clues and patterns and try to figure out what he is telling you.

Take time to watch your child closely. Think about what his behavior means. For example, is he having a tantrum because he is tired? Hungry? Frustrated? Overwhelmed? Understanding why he is behaving this way can help you figure out the best way to respond. Remember, it may take some trial and error to discover what works.

After a few minutes of a tickling game, Chrissy (4 months) frowns, turns away, and arches her back. Her dad, Peter, tickles her harder, trying to make her happy again, but Chrissy starts to cry. Dad stops the tickling.

Soon Chrissy calms down and smiles up at him. Peter realizes that when Chrissy turns her head and arches away from him, she is telling him that she has had enough and needs a break.

Understanding Your Child's Behavior

There are three factors that can help you understand the meaning of your child's behavior. They are like the pieces of a puzzle that you have to put together:

- **What's going on in your child's world?**

- **Age and stage of development**

- **Temperament**

What's Going on in Your Child's World?

Here are some questions to think about that might help you understand why your child is behaving a certain way:

- **Has your child been sick lately?**

- **Has anything changed in his daily routine?**

- **What is happening at home? How are family members getting along? Is someone sick who needs extra attention?**

- **Have there been other recent changes, such as a move, a loss in the family, or a new baby?**

- **Who is with your child when the behavior occurs? Where does the behavior take place?**

Here's how one mother tries to understand what's going on in her child's world:

Jessica, age 3, begins clinging to her mom at child care soon after the neighbor's dog dies. Jessica loved this dog. Her mother wonders if Jessica's clingy behavior is because she is now worried that people she loves might disappear too.

Age and Stage:
Your Child's Development

Knowing what to expect at different ages can help you figure out how to respond to your child. (See the development chart in the middle of the book. It will help you learn about the skills children are working on at different ages.)

For example, most children under age 3 are not able to control their desires or understand right from wrong. So when your child throws the ball inside—even though you have told him not to hundreds of times—he is not being "bad" on purpose. He is enjoying throwing. He is learning what he can do with balls. He doesn't need "punishment." He needs you to show him ways he *can* play with the ball.

Here are some thoughts to keep in mind:

- **Each child develops at his own pace.**
  There is a wide range of what is considered "normal." For example, one 8-month-old may be a great crawler. Another may not be crawling yet but can figure out how to get a pop up toy to work.

- **Sometimes when a child learns a new skill, he moves backward in another area.** For

example, a child who has just learned to walk may act more clingy than usual. A child who has just learned to use the potty may begin waking more at night. Don't worry, these changes are usually temporary.

- **Young children are developing many skills: thinking skills, social and emotional skills, physical skills, and language skills.** All these areas of development work together to help children grow and learn. For example, when a 9-month-old lifts both arms up to let her dad knows she wants to be picked up, all areas of development are at work.

She has the idea **(thinking skills)** that she wants to be picked up. So she lifts her arms up **(physical development)** to let her father know **(language/communication)** that she wants him—the person she loves and trusts—to pick her up **(social and emotional development)**.

Temperament:
What Is Your Child's Personal Style?

In the first chapter, you thought about your own temperament. Now, we focus on your child's temperament. Remember, your child's temperament is not something he chose or that you created. It is something he was born with. It affects the way he experiences the world.

Let's take a look at three different 2-year-olds arriving at the same child-care center.

Rahim looks around for a few seconds. He then rips off his coat and joins the children building with the blocks. Children like Rahim are comfortable in new situations and with new people.

Frank hangs onto his dad's leg and won't go into the room. He looks around for a few minutes and then takes his dad's hand. He walks to the puzzle table, sits down next to another child, and gets to work. Children like Frank are often cautious in new situations. They need support and time to feel safe and comfortable.

WHAT'S BEST FOR MY BABY AND ME?

Birth to 12 Months: Your Remarkable Baby

WHEN YOUR CHILD . . .	YOUR CHILD MIGHT BE SAYING:	WHAT YOU CAN DO:
. . . stops crying because she sees you coming.	I know I can count on you when I need you. I trust your love. Don't worry about spoiling me. When I get what I need when I need it, I feel good about myself and the people around me.	• Respond promptly when she cries. • Look for patterns in her cries and other cues. Is she tired? Wet? Hungry? Bored? Lonely? Overstimulated and in need of a break?
. . . cries, coos, gurgles, whimpers, smiles, rubs his eyes, arches his back, turns his head away, opens his eyes widely.	Watch me carefully! I communicate through cries, facial expressions, and movements when I'm sleepy, hungry, wet, frightened, bored, overwhelmed, or interested.	• Trust your instincts when you respond to your baby. His response will tell you if you're on target. If not, try something else.
. . . smiles and responds with pleasure when you talk, sing, or read to her.	I love it when we share words or songs. When I see how much fun words can be, it makes me want to keep "talking" and learning.	• Spend lots of time reading together. Let her choose the books, and explore them in any way she pleases. • Talk about what you are doing together.
. . . observes his own hands, pulls off your glasses, sticks his fingers in your nose, reaches for a toy, grabs the phone.	I am learning about how the world works and all of the things I can do with my own hands. I'm pretty amazing!	• Encourage his curiosity by offering safe objects to explore. • Guide his hands gently as he explores your face. • Share his excitement about new discoveries.
. . . breaks into tears when you arrive to pick him up from child care.	When I see you after a long day, I remember how much I've missed you. I save my most intense feelings for you because I trust you. You always come back.	• Don't rush out. Join in finishing what he was doing when you arrived. • Establish a "going home" ritual. Rituals are a comforting way to ease transitions.
. . . cries or clings to you when a new person approaches.	I don't know this person. I don't know what to expect from her, and that scares me.	• Give your child the space and time—in your arms or on your lap—to get used to new people. • Urge others to approach slowly. Have them break the ice by offering your child an interesting object

WHEN YOUR CHILD ...	YOUR CHILD MIGHT BE SAYING ...	WHAT YOU CAN DO ...
... clings or cries when you are leaving.	I love you. You make me feel safe. I don't want you to leave because I need you for so many things.	• Remind yourself that separations are difficult. • Play games such as peekaboo to prepare him for separation. • When you say, "Good-bye," calmly reassure him that you will always come back.
... says, "No!" and starts challenging rules and pushing limits.	I am a person with my own ideas. I am learning who I am and how to behave by trying out different ways and seeing which works best.	• Encourage independence with limited choices: "Red or blue sweater?" not "Which sweater?" • Establish consistent limits.
... sometimes act like he's going on 15 and at other times acts like a baby again.	I want to be grown-up and independent, but sometimes I get scared and need to know you're there for me. Try to be patient. This isn't easy for me, either!	• Be flexible. Support his independence, but let him revisit babyhood. • Let him help with real work, such as setting the table, so that he can feel "big." • Maintain special rituals from babyhood—for example, a bedtime routine.
... toddles over and grabs your legs after venturing off on his own.	No matter where I go, you'll always be there for me. You're my home base. I know I can always return to you.	• Greet your returning traveler with a big hug that lets him know you love him. • Play disappearing/reappearing games such as hide and seek. They will help him cope with separations.
... protests at bedtime.	There are too many exciting things going on for me to go to sleep. I want to be with you.	• Tell him when bedtime is approaching. • Establish a regular bedtime routine such as, bath, bed, books. • Give him a sense of control; let him pick the book or song.
... makes marks with crayons, stacks blocks, uses a spoon, drinks from a cup, and does other things to show off her small motor development.	I am learning to use my hands to explore and do things for myself. I'm so proud of what I can do! It keeps me occupied and helps me learn about all kinds of new things.	• Offer objects such as spoons, cups, and safe but small toys that give her a chance to practice using her fingers. • Teach her how meaningful her activities are. Send her scribbles in a letter to grandma. Have her help with cleaning up, now that she's able.
... points to something and then looks over to share her discovery with you.	Look at what I discovered. I want to see it or smell it or hold it. Can you get it for me so I can touch it, smell it, taste it?	• Talk about her discoveries and lift her to see, smell, or touch them. • If it's safe, offer her the object to explore.
... responds to music by dancing, moving, and brightening up.	This sounds great! I love to move, move, move!	• Join in, laugh, dance, have a great time. • Keep the music playing.

... Your Independent, Competent Toddler

WHEN YOUR CHILD...	YOUR CHILD MIGHT BE SAYING:	WHAT YOU CAN DO:
... plays pretend games with stuffed animals or make-believe toys such as telephones, stoves, cars, or dress-up clothes.	I'm practicing being a grown-up by doing things just like you. In my imagination, I can do anything and be anyone. That's the best part of play.	• Encourage imaginary play by providing lots of props and joining in. • Follow her lead and don't take over. You're a visitor in her world—she knows the rules!
... has a temper tantrum.	I've lost control. Maybe it's because I'm frustrated, tired, or angry. Or maybe I'm just overwhelmed by too much going on around me, and I need a break.	• Look for patterns to figure out what triggers his tantrums. • When it's over, put his feelings into words, and make a plan next time: "You got frustrated putting your shoe on. Next time you can ask for help."
... has trouble sharing or taking turns.	I'm beginning to learn that things aren't always the way I want them to be. It will take me a while and lots of practice to develop these skills.	• Let older toddlers try to work things out for themselves before stepping in to help. • Be their sharing coach. Help them take turns, but don't expect much. Toddlers are too young to master it.
... has trouble knowing when to stop.	I can't always put the brakes on when I am having a great time. Sometimes the things I'm doing are so-o-o exciting! With your help, I'll learn about self-control, but don't expect it to happen overnight.	• Establish clear rules and stick to them: "Balls are for outside." "All food and drinks at the table." Expect that he'll need reminders. • Always acknowledge when he shows self-control: "You remembered to bring your milk to the table. Good job!"
... tells you when his diaper is wet, or runs to the potty and sits on it fully clothed.	I know just what's happening in my body, and I'm thinking about starting to use this potty.	• Follow his lead. Forcing can lead to resistance and power struggles. • Expect lots of interest in potty activities, including company whenever you go to the bathroom. • Expect accidents, and never punish him for them.
... hits, pushes, or bites another child.	I'm angry, frustrated, or maybe just overexcited. I can't control myself. Help me, please!	• Watch for rising tension and signs of potential conflict. Step in before things get out of control. • Acknowledge feelings: "You're angry that Jake took your cookie." • Be clear about acceptable behavior: "It's okay to be angry, but it's not okay to hit."

Carlos speeds into the room ahead of his grandmother—no time to waste. He charges up to two boys who are pushing fire trucks and making siren sounds. Carlos grabs one of the trucks and yells, "MINE!" Children like Carlos tend to be "big reactors." They are exciting and passionate but can have a difficult time controlling their strong feelings and desires.

Five Aspects of Temperament

Below are five factors to look at to understand your child's temperament:

1. Intensity level

2. Activity level

3. Frustration level

4. Reaction to new people

5. Reaction to change

As you think about your child's temperament, remember, there is no good or bad or right or wrong way for a child to be. But let's face it, some temperaments are more of a challenge. For example, it takes a lot of energy and patience to parent a child who is very intense and has big reactions.

Intensity Level:

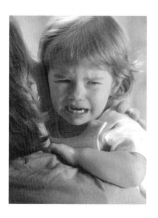

Intensity level describes how strongly your child reacts to different experiences. For example, one baby whines when she is angry. Another screams her head off. One child doesn't seem to notice when a fire truck passes. Another child starts crying. It's too much for him. Most children have reactions that fall somewhere in the middle.

Think about how intensely your child reacts

- How does your child usually react to what he sees, hears, touches, smells, and tastes?

- Does your child express her feelings with high, medium, or low intensity?

- How often do you find yourself helping your child calm down? How much help does your child need to calm down?

How would you rate your child's intensity level?

Your Child's Intensity Level
1 . . . . 2 . . . . 3 . . . . 4 5
Low intensity   High intensity

Ways to support your child

For a low intensity child:

- Follow your child's interests. Join in his play.
- Engage your child. For example, use different voices to get his attention when reading a book.

For a high intensity child:

- Let her know that you understand her feelings.
- Stay calm when she is "losing it."
- Help her learn to calm herself.

Activity Level:

Activity level describes how active your child is. Some kids seem to move nonstop. Some prefer to explore by watching and using their hands, rather than their whole body. Most kids fall somewhere in between.

Think about your child's activity level

- What are your child's favorite activities?

- How often do you find yourself saying things like "slow down," "take it easy," and "let's take a break"?

- How does your child respond when her movement is limited—when she is told, for example, not to crawl on the grocery store floor?

How would you rate your child's activity level?

Your Child's Activity Level

1 . . . . 2 . . . . 3 . . . . 4 5
Sitter   Mover and shaker

Ways to support your child

For a less active child:

- Give him lots of chances to play with the things he enjoys—like books, puzzles, and blocks.

- Encourage some active play. Have a toddler act out a story you are reading together. Listen to music and dance!

For a more active child:

- Offer lots of chances for safe, active play.

- Have realistic expectations. Let her get up from the table when she is finished eating. Let her "move and shake" as you read to her.

Frustration

Level:

MARILYN NOLT

Frustration level describes how your child handles things that frustrate him, such as a puzzle piece that won't fit or a zipper that is stuck. Some children can handle a lot of frustration. Some get frustrated very easily. Most fall somewhere in the middle. Keep in mind that a child's ability to handle frustration can depend on certain factors such as how hard the task is and if she is hungry or tired.

Think about how easily your child gets frustrated

- How often does your child get frustrated? A lot? Rarely? Sometimes?

- Are there times he gets frustrated more easily—like when he is hungry or tired at the end of a very busy day?

How would you rate your child's way of dealing with frustration?

Your Child's Frustration Level

1 . . . . 2 . . . . 3 . . . . 4 5
"I give up"   "I'll try again"

Ways to support your child

For a child who is easily frustrated:

- Let her know you understand her frustration. "You are angry that the bear won't fit in this puzzle space! Silly bear!" Using humor can often be very helpful.

- Be your child's coach. Help her think through the problem to find a solution.

- Be a role model. When *you* face a problem, stay calm.

For a child who keeps on trying:

- Offer him new challenges.

- Let him know everybody needs help some-times. It is difficult for some children to ask for help when they need it.

Reaction
to New People:

Reaction to new people describes how your child responds when she meets someone new. Some children love to meet new people. Some are very fearful and cautious. Most children fall somewhere in between.

How would you rate your child's approach to new people?

Your Child's Approach to New People

1 . . . . 2 . . . . 3 . . . . 4 5
"Let's take it slow"   "Glad to meet you"

Ways to support your child

For a child who is slow to warm-up:

- Help your child feel safe. Hold her in your arms or hold her hand when she meets new people. Stay close to your child until she is comfortable with a new person.

- Show positive feelings toward new people. Your child reads your cues too!

For a child who is eager to meet new people:

- Give her lots of chances to meet others. Take trips to the playground and library.

- Help her learn to be a good friend. All children need help sometimes learning to share, to settle an argument, or to say "sorry."

Reaction to Change:

Reaction to change describes how your child adjusts to changes, such as a new classroom at child care or even a change in his regular chair at the dinner table. Some children don't mind change much at all. Some have a very hard time with change. Most fall somewhere in the middle.

Think about how your child handles change

- How does your child react to change?

- How easy is it for you to help your child move from one activity to the next, for example, when going from bath to bed or from park to home?

How would you rate your child's response to change?

Your Child's Response to Change

1 . . . . 2 . . . . 3 . . . . 4 5
"I like things the way they are"   "Bring on something new"

Ways to support your child

For a child who has a hard time with change:

- Let your child know about changes before they happen. "After this book is finished, it's time for bed."

- Have your child bring something familiar to a new place. Going to the doctor or a new child-care center will be less scary if your child can hold his favorite stuffed animal or blanket.

For a child who is comfortable with change:

- Offer your child a variety of new experiences.

- Be sensitive to your child's behavior. Some changes can be difficult for even the most easygoing child.

REMEMBER

- Parenting is like being a detective. Watching your child's behavior gives you important clues about what he is thinking and feeling.

- Understanding your child's behavior involves putting together the pieces of a puzzle: what is going on in his world, his stage of development, and his temperament.

Step **3**

Making Good Decisions

You've taken Step 1 and thought about yourself.
You've taken Step 2 and thought about your child.
Step 3 puts it all together and uses what you've
learned to make good parenting decisions.

Using What You Know About Yourself and Your Child to Help Your Child Grow

Use the scales on the next page to see how you and
your child are alike and different. For each temperament characteristic, draw a circle to show where you
see your child on the continuum. Then mark an "X"
to show where you see yourself.

Here is an example of how to use the scale.

Intensity of reaction:

1 . . . . X2 . . . . . . 3 . . . . . . (4) 5

Even tempered/laid-back   Big reactor

You may also want to have other adults in your child's life place themselves on these scales. (Use a different mark to note where each adult is on each scale.)

TEMPERAMENT SCALE

Intensity of reaction

1 . . . . . . 2 . . . . . 3 . . . . . . 4 5

Low intensity   High intensity

Activity level

1 . . . . . . 2 . . . . . 3 . . . . . . 4 5

Sitter   Mover and shaker

Frustration level

1 . . . . . . 2 . . . . . 3 . . . . . . 4 5

"I give up"   "I'll try again"

Reaction to new people

1 . . . . . . 2 . . . . . . 3 . . . . . . 4 5

"Let's take it slow"   "Glad to meet you"

Response to change

1 . . . . . . 2 . . . . . . 3 . . . . . . 4 5

"I like things the way they are"   "Bring on something new"

What do you think?:

- How are you and your child alike? How does this affect your relationship?

- How are you and your child different? How does this affect your relationship?

Your child needs you to understand and adapt to his style as much as you can. Why? It helps him to:

- feel loved and important

- trust you

- feel good about himself

Making Everyday Decisions

Let's look at how Stacy and Ed use the three-step approach to decide how to set limits for their son, Robbie.

*S*tacy and Ed both work outside the home. Their son, Robbie, is 22 months old. He wants to do everything by himself—feed himself, pour his milk, walk the dog. He shouts, hits, and throws things when he is frustrated that he can't do it "by myself!"

Stacy is always in a power struggle with Robbie. She has taken away special toys and TV time and put him in time-outs. Nothing works. Ed finds it easier to deal with Robbie.

The Problem: How to Set Limits

Using what they know about themselves (Step 1) and Robbie (Step 2), Stacy and Ed come up with some ideas for setting limits (Step 3).

STEP ONE:
What Stacy and Ed Know About Themselves

- We love Robbie with all our hearts.

- We need to have more time and energy for Robbie.

- Stacy gets upset when things feel out of control

- Stacy gets easily drawn into power struggles with Robbie.

- We are worried about letting Robbie do things by himself because of the mess it will create.

STEP TWO: What Stacy and Ed Know About Robbie	STEP THREE: What Ed and Stacy Are Going to Try
Robbie has lots of good qualities, such as his passion for life. Robbie needs to get more attention when he is cooperating.	• Remind ourselves of all of Robbie's wonderful qualities. • Praise Robbie when he is well- behaved.
Robbie is not hyperactive. He just likes to move!	• Be sure Robbie has some time each day to play outside. • Find ways Robbie can play safely but actively in the house.
Robbie needs the adults around him to stay calm when he is upset. This will help him calm down more easily.	• Show Robbie that we understand his feelings. For example, by telling him, "It makes you so-o-o-o angry when you can't get your shoe on!" • Give Robbie choices, within limits. "Would you like to carry the napkins or the spoons to the table?" • Stacy will work on staying calm when Robbie is losing it. • Ed will step in to help more often.
The power struggles are not good for Robbie (or Mom)! Nobody wins. And it doesn't help Robbie learn the limits.	• Work on being more clear and consistent with limits. • Show Robbie what he *can* do. • Reduce power struggles.

Robbie likes to do things himself. It makes him feel confident about his abilities. But he still needs help. This is hard for him to accept.	• Think of ways Robbie can practice his new skills safely and without making a mess, such as:
	  —Let him pour his own milk. Do it over the sink to reduce spills.
	  —Give him lots of containers and toys to play with in the bathtub so he can experiment with water without a mess.
	  —Let him walk the dog if one of us holds the leash with him.

Coping When Nothing Works

Sometimes nothing works! No one has all the answers. But when you keep on trying, and don't give up, you let your child know he can trust you and that he is not alone. This will make him feel secure, lovable, confident, and good about himself.

REMEMBER

- No matter what your similarities and differences are, your child needs you to try your best to understand and adjust to her style.

- Appreciate and enjoy your child for who he is. This will make him feel secure, lovable, confident, and good about himself.

- The three-step approach can be applied to almost any parenting challenge you face.

Final Thoughts

Some parents wonder whether using these three steps to make decisions is a full-time job. Don't worry. Over time, this approach will become a natural part of your thinking process. You may not have time or it may not be your style to go through all of the steps like the parents mentioned earlier. That's okay. Just being aware of the steps can help you stop and think before you act. Doing this will help you make better decisions and be the best parent you can be.

About the Authors

Claire Lerner, LCSW-C, is a licensed clinical social worker, child development specialist, and Director of Parenting Resources at ZERO TO THREE. Ms. Lerner writes a regular column on young children's behavior for **American Baby Magazine** and she is the co-author of ZERO TO THREE's best-selling parent book, **Learning & Growing Together**.

Ms. Lerner has been a practicing clinician for 20 years, providing parent education and counseling services to families with children of all ages. She also trains early childhood professionals and pediatricians on early childhood development and building strong relationships with parents.

Amy Laura Dombro, MS, is the former head of the Infant and Family Center at Bank Street College of Education in New York City. She currently consults with and writes for a variety of national organizations including ZERO TO THREE. She is co-author of **Learning & Growing Together** and **The Ordinary Is Extraordinary: How Children Under Three Learn**.